LIVING AND NON-LIVING

Rainforest

Cassie Mayer

www.heinemann.co.uk/library

Visit our website to find out more information about Heinemann Library books.

To order:
- ☎ Phone 44 (0) 1865 888066
- 🖹 Send a fax to 44 (0) 1865 314091
- 🖥 Visit the Heinemann Bookshop at www.heinemann.co.uk/library to browse our catalogue and order online.

First published in Great Britain by Heinemann Library, Halley Court, Jordan Hill, Oxford OX2 8EJ, part of Harcourt Education. Heinemann is a registered trademark of Harcourt Education Ltd.

Editorial: Cassie Mayer and Diyan Leake
Design: Kimberly Miracle
Illustration: Mark Beech
Picture research: Erica Martin and Melissa Allison
Production: Duncan Gilbert

Originated by Modern Age
Printed and bound in China by South China Printing Co. Ltd

ISBN 978 0 431 18461 6
12 11 10 09 08
10 9 8 7 6 5 4 3 2 1

British Library Cataloguing in Publication Data
Mayer, Cassie
   Living and Non-living: Rainforest

A full catalogue record for this book is available from the British Library.

Acknowledgements
The publishers would like to thank the following for permission to reproduce photographs: Alamy p. **19** (Gary Howell); Corbis p. **5** (Tom Bean), **11** (Royalty Free), **15**, **18** (Envision), **21** (Bob Krist), **23** (stream: Royalty Free), **back cover** (Royalty Free); FLPA pp. **4** (Minden Pictures), **6** (Minden Pictures/JH Editorial/ Cyril Ruoso), **7** (Minden Pictures/Pete Oxford), **8** (Minden Pictures), **9** (Minden Pictures), **12** (Minden Pictures), **13** (Minden Pictures), **14** (Minden Pictures), **16** (David Hosking), **23** (rainforest trees: Minden Pictures); Getty Images pp. **22** (Carlos Navajas), **23** (rainforest: Carlos Navajas); Nature Picture Library pp. **17** (Pete Oxford), **20** (Ingo Arndt); NHPA p. **10**.

Cover photograph of a toucan in Brazil reproduced with permission of Getty Images/Photodisc Red (John Wang).

Every effort has been made to contact copyright holders of any material reproduces in this book. Any omissions will be rectified in subsequent printings if notice is given to the publisher.

Contents

A rainforest habitat

A rainforest is an area of land.
A rainforest can be warm and wet.

A rainforest has living things.
A rainforest has non-living things.

Monkey

howler monkey

Is a monkey a living thing?

Does a monkey need food? *Yes.*
Does a monkey need water? *Yes.*

Does a monkey need air? *Yes.*

Does a monkey grow? *Yes.*

So a monkey is a living thing.

Stream

Is a stream a living thing?

Does a stream need food? *No.*
Does a stream need more water? *No.*

Does a stream need air? *No.*

Does a stream grow? *No.*

So a stream is not a living thing.

Tree

Is a tree a living thing?

Does a tree need food? *Yes*.
Does a tree need water? *Yes*.

Does a tree need air? *Yes.*

Does a tree grow? *Yes.*

So a tree is a living thing.

Butterfly

Is a butterfly a living thing?

nectar – butterfly food

Does a butterfly need food? *Yes*.
Does a butterfly need water? *Yes*.

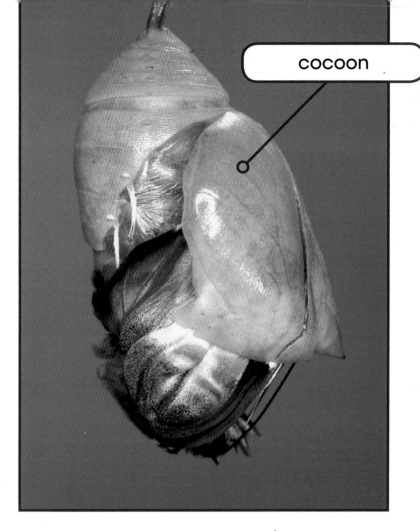

cocoon

Does a butterfly need air? *Yes.*

 Does a butterfly grow? *Yes.*

So a butterfly is a living thing.

A rainforest is home to many things.
A rainforest is an important habitat.

Picture glossary

habitat area where plants and animals live

rainforest a habitat that can be warm and wet

stream small body of flowing water

Index

Notes for parents and teachers
Before reading
Talk to the children about rainforests. Have they seen them in books or on the TV? Talk about how lots of things grow in a rainforest because it is very warm and wet. Show the children a map or globe and point out the largest areas of rainforests.
After reading
Cut out pictures of things such as a cat, dog, tree, book, house, flower, and car. Ask the children to answer the key questions to determine if the thing is living or non-living (needs food, water, and air, and it grows). Help them to sort the pictures into two piles. Write "Living" and "Non-living" at the top of two sheets of paper. Ask the children to stick the pictures on the correct sheet.